D0938908

GARDENS *of* KENTUCKY

Photography by Dan Dry

Text by Amy Spears

Gardens *of* Kentucky

No occupation is so delightful to me
As the culture of the earth
And no culture comparable
To that of the garden.

Thomas Jefferson

GARDENS *of* KENTUCKY

Photography by

DAN DRY

Text by

AMY SPEARS

THE SULGRAVE PRESS

Contents

The Gardeners

Helen Harting Abell, Louisville

Mr. and Mrs. Joseph Ardery, Louisville

Charles and Anne Arnsberg, Old Louisville

Howard and Laurie Bledsoe, Old Louisville

Laura Lee Brown and Steve Wilson, Louisville

Mr. and Mrs. Owsley Brown, Louisville

Mr. and Mrs. James Brammer, Ashland

Mr. and Mrs. John W. D. Bowling, Danville

Mrs. Thomas Bullitt, Louisville

Mr. and Mrs. William Dyer, Paducah

Mr. and Mrs. Stephen Clymer, Paducah

Mr. William C. Creason, General Manager, Labrot
      & Graham Distillery, Woodford County

Mr. and Mrs. James Drury, Hopkinsville

Mr. and Mrs. David Eager, Louisville

Mr. and Mrs. Cecil Fannin, Jr., Ashland

Mrs. Judy Ferrell, Bourbon County

Mr. and Mrs. Robert Garey, Paducah

Mr. and Mrs. John Grubbs, Danville

Mr. and Mrs. Paul Grumley, Paducah

Mr. and Mrs. Ian Henderson, Glenview

Messrs. Billy Hertz and Tom Schnapp, Louisville

Mr. and Mrs, Henning Hilliard, Louisville

Mrs. Henry Holliday, Lexington

Dr. and Mrs. W. Mack Jackson, Boyle County

Ms. Lowrey Jackson, Boyle County

Dr. and Mrs. Lawrence Jelsma, Shelby County

Mr. and Mrs. Gene Katterjohn, Paducah

Mr. and Mrs. Robert Kulp, Louisville

Diane and Gary Klier, Old Louisville

Mr. and Mrs. John Lenihan, Glenview

Mr. and Mrs. Fairleigh Lussky, Louisville

Dr. and Mrs. John Lacy, Danville

Mr. and Mrs. Ben Matthews, Shelby County

Mrs. C. King McClure, Louisville

Mr. William L. McMahan, Glenview

Mr. and Mrs. Leland Marret, Middletown

Mr. and Mrs. Sam Miller, Louisville

Gordon Moffett and Leah Stewart, Old Louisville

Mr. and Mrs. Louis Myre, Paducah

Mr. and Mrs. Robert Nash, Oldham County

Mrs. Carlile Nichols, Danville

Mr. and Mrs. William Paxton, Paducah

Mr. Craig Pearl, Old Louisville

Mrs. Ceci Perry, Lexington

Ms. Frederika Petter, Paducah

Ms. Lois Ann Polan, Lexington

Mr. and Mrs. Carl Pollard, Oldham County

Mr. and Mrs. Junius W. Prince III, Louisville

Mrs. Robert McDowell Rodes, Lexington

Mr. and Mrs. John Ross, Ashland

Mrs. William Samuels, Louisville

Mrs. Peter Spalding, Louisville

Ms. Irene Spicer, Old Louisville

Mr. and Mrs. William Tate, Louisville

Ms. Brenda Van Hoose, Paris

The Wallis House, Paris

Messrs. Tim Warton and Joe Jarboe, Old Louisville

Mr. and Mrs. Marion Webb, Louisville

Mr. and Mrs. Robert Webb, Paducah

Mr. and Mrs. James Welch, Prospect

Ms. Ellen Workman, Hopkinsville

Dr. and Mrs. Jesse Wright, Louisville

Ms. Dawn Yates, Louisville

Introduction

The gardens of Kentucky are as varied as the diverse topography of the state, extending from the mountains of the east to the broad plains of the west. Where the great gardens in other parts of America have flourished for many years, climatic conditions are generally consistent and predictable. Such will never be the fate of gardeners in Kentucky, who battle drought and deluge, desert heat, arctic freezes and erratic weather patterns woven together by prolonged periods of high Ohio Valley humidity. Behind every beautiful Kentucky garden stands a determined and canny practitioner.

From precise *parterres* to meandering paths, the gardens of Kentucky reflect styles from the most formal European to the most inventive in contemporary design. Garden clubs throughout the state have saved historic gardens, revitalized neglected plans and revived interest in one of mankind's earliest art forms, the garden. It is, however, the individual gardener who is able "to see the world in a grain of sand" and cajole *terra* to cooperate with *flora*, thereby fashioning plants, flowers, shrubs and trees into art.

While some gardens strictly adhere to a definite style, others draw on elements from a number of traditions. Therefore, some of the gardens in this book defy categorization and are included in several sections.

Grandes Dames

Some of the creators of these lovely Kentucky gardens are no longer with us, but their gardens live on, tended and expanded by family members or new owners. These grand gardens were originally designed in an age of abundant and knowledgeable labor. The fact that they continue to thrive is testament to the power which their beauty exerts over those who come in contact with it. Few have been able to resist perpetuating the designs of Frederick Law Olmstead, Mary Louise Speed and Anne Bruce Haldeman.

Jewels of the Realm

Other gardens are on a smaller scale, and it is here that the personalities of their owners are even more evident. The inviting gate, the sunken terrace, the fanciful garden ornament and the reflecting pool all speak to the unique and fascinating tastes of their creators. Asking the daughter of one of these gardeners why her mother undertook such an enormous task, she replied, " she loved being frustrated." Happily and intriguingly, we see expressed in these gardens the sense of humor as well as the sense of determination of the owners.

Amid Terraces and Beyond Walls

Today, it is rare that gardeners enjoy unlimited space in which to work their special art. More often than not, particularly with houses built in the past fifty years, the house was designed without a garden. Given this scenario, the garden, rather than evolving from the land, has had to conform to what remained after the house was constructed. Terracing is but one manner of carving out a salubrious space for flowers, trees, and lawn. The effect of walls and stairways and paths can be quite enchanting, and the resulting vistas give new dimensions to the dwelling. These gardens often become extensions of the living spaces of the house.

Bare to Blooming

Among the most remarkable gardens are those which are created, literally, from scratch. With the development of suburbia, rectangular lots were laid out, often ignoring the lay of the land. Soil compacted by heavy machinery has had to be enriched and lightened before miracles can take place. Gardeners who can look at a flat

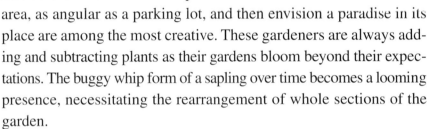

area, as angular as a parking lot, and then envision a paradise in its place are among the most creative. These gardeners are always adding and subtracting plants as their gardens bloom beyond their expectations. The buggy whip form of a sapling over time becomes a looming presence, necessitating the rearrangement of whole sections of the garden.

Country Gardens

Nothing can be more challenging than vast expanses of space, and that is the agony and the ecstasy of the country gardener. To prevent the area from being dwarfed by the scale of the surrounding landscape, the garden often functions as a bridge between the personal scale of the house and its inhabitants and the vistas beyond. The country gardener must also contend with what seems like legions of moles, raccoons, and deer. In the country, pest control becomes an art form.

Urban and Suburban Landscapes

The urban gardener struggles with ubiquitous squirrels as well as the man made problems of noise and pollution. Space is limited, soil of poor quality and daylight is often fleeting as the encroachment of neighboring buildings deny the city garden its full share of sun. Despite these obstacles to horticultural excellence and creativity, urban gardens provide unexpected pleasures in areas dense with asphalt, concrete and glass towers. Nothing can compare to stepping from a hot, busy street into the lush coolness of a city garden.

Grandes Dames

Allées, parterres, and graceful pools are some of the hallmarks of these grand gardens. Reflecting the European influences of symmetry and stylized plantings, these gardens hark back to an age of order and elegance.

Following the design of Bryant Fleming of New York, the Samuels garden, with its manicured paths and precise borders, is European in feel.

The garden of Laurice Samuels in Louisville has flourished under her guidance for the last 54 years. Laid out along formal lines, the colorful flower beds and handsome garden ornaments lead the eye from one focal point to another.

(Left) The European lindens form a green vault above the pea gravel walk, dappling the path with sunbeams in the Samuels garden.

The perfectly clipped yew hedges provide a fitting backdrop for the flower beds and the graceful artillery at their center.

A pair of ornamental cranes enjoy a stroll in the Samuels garden.

(Overleaf) In Louisville, the formal gardens at Whitehall, formerly the Hume Logan home, have been revitalized by the Historic Homes Foundation, Inc. which has extended and expanded the existing plan.

The paved walk which runs the length of the Whitehall garden transports the visitor between the seasonal borders to an apse-shaped wall and its inviting benches.

(Below) Graceful arches provide a verdant rhythm in the Whitehall garden.

A lion stands guard at the garden of Mr. and Mrs. John Lenihan in Glenview.

(Right) Intricate wrought iron gateposts mark the entrance to the Lenihan garden.

The Governor's Mansion in Frankfort overlooks the reflecting pool and the
very formal *parterres* of boxwood hedges and vibrant begonia beds. The
Capitol is in the background.

The Mansion rises above the stylized French gardens.

Three cherubs play above the sparkling water on a very hot summer's day at the Capitol. The garden was designed when the Mansion was built in 1914, but not planted until 1980. Frederick Law Olmstead created some of the original landscaping around the capitol grounds.

(Left) Oxmoor, located in eastern Jefferson County, was part of a 1785 land grant and has remained in the Bullitt family since that time. The gardens are very English in feel and are laid out along perpendicular axes. The bright annuals in the borders in the central garden create a rhythm that draws the eye toward the far end of the garden. Marian Cruger Coffin, one of the architects of Winterthur gardens in Delaware, designed the garden around 1911.

(Above) The most recent addition to the Oxmoor garden is the rockery which features ornamental grasses and conifers enlivened by statuary.

(Above) The dramatic *allée* of majestic oaks and other trees is a fitting introduction to Oxmoor and its gardens.

(Opposite page) At Oxmoor the wisteria-covered mahogany arbor, one of a pair, frames the gazebo at the end of the path. Stone-lined paths wander through beds of plantings and across a timbered bridge. An inviting branch bench nestles among the hostas close to the spring house.

Visitors follow a handsome brick walk into a charming side garden whose focal point is a gleaming white gazebo.

One of the salient features of the Oxmoor rockery is this flagstone-lined pool.

Circles within circles define the perfection of the round pool, the lawn and the bordering beds which frame
this part of the Oxmoor garden.

The contrast of the shady pool and the sunlit lawn beyond lends additional interest to the structure of this garden.

The family's golden retriever finds the pool a particularly inviting spot.

This garden in Jefferson County was originally designed by Arthur W. Cowell of the State College of Pennsylvania in 1927. The terrace which runs the length of the back of the house overlooks the formal garden. Bounded on one side by a handsome arbor, the garden centers on a lovely reflecting pool surrounded by ivy.

Ashland, the home of the famed Henry Clay, is located in Lexington. Its glorious Italianate plan has been carefully restored. The garden's formal *parterres* and magnificent clipped boxwoods are linked by a number of paths.

A corner of Ashland may be glimpsed through the lush foliage of the boxwoods in the garden and the towering trees which surround the historic home.

Little Cote, the Louisville home of David and Susan Eager, was for many years the home of Mr. and Mrs. Archibald Cochran. In 1935, Mrs. Cochran began the garden in keeping with the design by Bryant Fleming of New York. The boxwood hedges which give the garden its structure are clipped in the shape of clouds.

Jewels of the Realm

Scattered throughout the state, these gardens are delightful in their unique detail and marvelous designs. They have grown in stature with years of care, guided by unwavering vision by their creators and owners.

The sinuous curve of the flowering border in the Glenview garden of Mr. and Mrs. Ian Henderson is one of its most attractive elements.

One of Paducah's loveliest gardens is that of Mr. and Mrs. Stephen Clymer. The perpendicular brick walks intersect at the sundial set in a bed of ivy.

The enticing garden path with its boxwood
sentries leads to the edge of the elegant pool
of Mr. and Mrs. Louis Myre in Paducah.

Mr. and Mrs Ian Henderson of Glenview removed a tennis court to make room for their gardens. Entering the small garden from the sunporch, the visitor looks across the expanse of the lawn to a pair of crescent shaped beds in the distance.

A brick walk leads to a charming bench, a perfect spot from which to enjoy the intricacies of the Henderson's garden.

(Above) Dogwood Hill, the house and garden of Laura Lee Brown and her husband, Steve Wilson, has found new life. The pleasing, personal scale of the garden is enlivened by the selection and placement of unique statues and sculptures. The gate designed by Scott Tichenor opens onto the lawn and gardens.

The statue of a woman, created by sculptor Marvin Hirn, sits in a circlet of liviope at Dogwood Hill.

38

The Louis Myre garden in Paducah is one of the loveliest in the state. A perfect place to enjoy the view is from the chaise underneath a flower-laden trellis.

A cool path in the Myre garden leads past an ivy-covered wall to an arched opening.

Brick steps with their green stair rods lead down into the garden originally
designed by Mary Louise Speed.

Over 50 years old, a climbing hydrangea scales the chimney of this Georgian home in Jefferson County.

(Both pages) Cave Hill Cemetery, established in 1848, is located in the Highlands in Louisville. Recognized as a national arboretum and botanical garden, Cave Hill is one of the most beautiful spots in Louisville, particularly in the spring when the dogwoods burst into bloom.

A narrow space along the edge of Mary Webb's driveway
became the site of a glorious perennial border.

Amid Terraces and Behind Walls

A flat or difficult landscape achieves depth and
interest when terraces are carved into the land.
An ever-changing viewpoint is but one of the
advantages of terracing. However, nothing is
more intriguing than a wall pierced by a gate.
The urge to enter is irresistible.

The home of Mr. and
Mrs. Marion Webb
posed new opportuni-
ties for Mary, a
popular and talented
garden designer in
Louisville.

The terrace of the Webb's garden features a fountain mounted on a wall of ivy. Mr. Webb devised a delicate spray which continually mists the ivy.

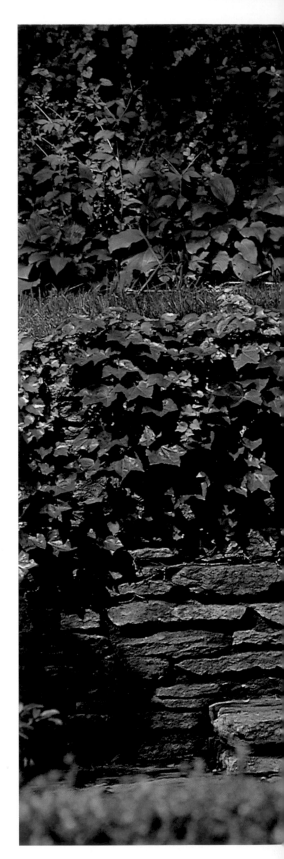

An unusual feature of the Fairleigh Lusskey garden in Louisville is the placement of the brick path. On the upper terrace, the path with its sitting areas runs
behind the flower borders, not in front as is more commonplace, allowing a
visitor to admire the garden and terraces below.

The serendipity of the David Eager garden is a cool seat flanked by guardian
angels and magnolias.

Set in the lower terrace of Abby and Fairleigh Lusskey's garden are several large granite stones used years ago for grinding paint pigment. This terrace affords a lovely view of the house and gardens above.

The brick terraces with their black wrought iron railings and brass finials provide a number of graceful entrances into Ellen Tate's garden.

(Below) A curving path of paving stones winds through the shade garden which emerges onto the emerald lawn at the Tates.

48

Ellen Tate meticulously restored the ham house, transforming it into a beguiling playhouse for her grandchildren.

The terrace of Mrs. Peter Spalding, Jr. overlooks an enchanting, winding garden path.

Abby Lussky's garden in Louisville unfolds on several levels. Terracing seemed to be the only way to create sufficient space for her many ideas.

Helen Harting Abell has created a series of three interconnected terraces which are extensions of the rooms of her Louisville home. A boxwood hedge encloses this terrace and creates a living wall behind the rose garden.

The garden of Vicki Prince in Louisville hardly needs a sign to mark its presence. The genesis of this garden began after a tornado in 1974 decimated the entire neighborhood. Originally surrounded by a chain link fence and with only one tree left standing, Vicki has created a place of rare beauty.

From Bare To Blooming

These gardeners have never seen a patch of earth they didn't like. No matter how resistant the soil or uninspiring the space, they have used their wisdom and their wiles to bring forth beauty where none previously existed.

The Prince sun garden has completely taken over one side of the yard.
Each end of this border is anchored by majestic stands of yellow iris.

Everywhere the eye falls in the Prince garden, there is something in bloom.

A weathered garden nymph oversees Vicki's prodigious effort, but as she remarks, "To me, working is the enjoyment."

Dr. and Mrs. Jesse Wright inherited a deep backyard with a pool in its midst and some overgrown taxus hedges.
Dr. Wright has tamed the landscape and sculpted a lovely garden in its place.

(Above and below) The Wright's garden was the spectacular setting of their son's wedding. Dr. Wright grew up gardening with his grandmother and has included many "old fashioned" plants in his garden.

Canary Cottage, the Ceci Perry home in Lexington, seems to float above its colorful front garden.

The garden of Mr. and Mrs. Joseph G. Thomas in Louisville found its beginnings in a bare, steeply sloped back yard. Under Barbie Thomas's direction, it now boasts terracing, lovely plantings and stately trees.

As the trees have matured in the Thomas garden, Barbie has become increasingly knowledgeable about shade-loving plants.

This very unusual gate at the Thomases opens into a small side garden.

Ceci Perry's Lexington home is called Canary Cottage, but when she first moved in, there was nothing on which even the smallest bird could perch. With the help of garden designer Ezra Haggard, Ceci has transformed the pie-shaped lot into a verdant spot.

A study in different shades and textures of green draws attention to this area in the Perry garden.

The side entrance to Margaret and Robert Kulp's garden in Louisville is through this rustic gate.

The constantly evolving Kulp garden has been three decades in the making. The daylilies and astilbe have blossomed into a lovely bouquet.

Country Gardens

Many of the state's country gardens are rapidly being surrounded by urban sprawl, making their very existence even more precious. The original gardens in the country were strictly utilitarian as they provided vegetables and fruits for the entire household. Located relatively close to the house, these gardens slowly became more refined. The addition of herb beds and more formal plantings increased as survival became less of a struggle.

Standing on the brick terrace of Longfield, the farm of Mr. and Mrs. Robert Nash in Oldham County, the eye follows the graceful curve of the lawn.

Thoroughbreds graze beyond the Nash's well-ordered vegetable garden.

The Nash family in Oldham County has enjoyed many a pleasant afternoon in this pavilion overlooking the garden.

A lovely weathered bench nestles into the garden border, inviting visitors to sit and watch the world go by.

(Left) The sundial stands sentinel over not only the sunny days but also the countless hours of hard work that go into maintaining the Nash garden. The bower beyond offers a shady vantage point. (Above and below) Their home overlooks the borders and lush lawns which draw the visitor through the garden.

Eastern Jefferson County is home to the garden of Mr. and Mrs. Leland Marret. It began as a large bare area around the house with a few large trees as the only plantings but is now landscaped with masses of flowers. The Marrets offer a number of spots from which to admire the garden. Mr. Marret is an accomplished woodworker who designed and built the handsome fence and arched gate around the formal garden.

(Right) Mary Marret has tucked a statue here and a bird bath there, inviting the eye to linger a little while longer.

Large trees in the pasture lean over the Marret's fence, contrasting their shade to the color and light of the flower border beneath them.

The Welch garden, with its widely spaced and well-ordered rows, boasts lovely gladioli and peonies.

(Left) Cardinal Hill, the home of Mr. and Mrs. James Welch in Prospect, has a large cutting garden from which Jane Welch creates her beautiful flower arrangements.

A half-opened gate at the bottom of the Henning Hilliard garden opens into the meadow beyond.

(Left and below): Stockdale, built in 1832 by Governor Isaac Shelby's daughter, is located in Shelby County and is owned by Dr. and Mrs. Lawrence Jelsma. The beautiful and very old trees shade a comfortable bench and frame a row of plantings along a white four-rail fence.

In keeping with the historic past of Stockdale is this herb and perennial garden planted by the Jelsmas. The limestone bird bath at its center was carved by Kentucky artist Don Lawer.

(Right) The dry wall fence is a distinctive characteristic of the garden of Dr. and Mrs. W. Mack Jackson in Boyle County. This type of fence is prominent in Central Kentucky and was built by Irish laborers in the early 1800s. Dr. Jackson constructed all of the fences on his farm. Boxwoods and moss lined brick paths provide the garden's structure.

(Below) A curved bench overlooks Gerry Jackson's garden and the fields beyond the stone fence.

Raindrops cling to the daylilies bordering the fence at Ferrellmont, the home of Judy Ferrell, in Bourbon County.

The greenhouse at Ferrellmont overlooks the fields as well as the house's garden.

Woodford County is home to Lane's End, one of Kentucky's most beautiful thoroughbred farms. Owned by Mr. and Mrs. Will Farish, the house amid its gardens is in perfect harmony with gently rolling countryside. Queen Elizabeth and President Bush have both been guests at the famous farm.

The old farm wagon at Lane's End is transformed into a stylish flower cart.

Elegant in their simplicity, these gates mark the entrance to the Farish farm.

The perennial border echoes the graceful curve of the Lane's End pool terrace and the soft rise of the hill beyond.

The well-ordered greenhouse provides seasonal flowers for the garden and the house.

The wide green path seamlessly flows through the woods toward the house at Lane's End.

Hermitage Farm in Oldham County is an historic thoroughbred farm belonging to Mr. and Mrs. Carl Pollard. The house was built in the early 1830s, but the garden is a recent addition. Bebe Pollard has created a border garden which serves as a transition between the pool and the house.

The view from the pool encompasses the garden, the ornamental fruit trees and the back of Hermitage.

The garden of Mr. and Mrs. James Brammer in Ashland melds the nearby woodlands into the overall design.

The wood stairsteps in the Brammer garden are so natural and unobtrusive that they appear to have grown in place.

The terrace at the Brammer's is reached by a series of wide graceful steps and landings.

Mr. and Mrs. William Hoke Camp's garden in Oldham County presents itself in well-ordered rows and a series of garden rooms. These magnificent sunflowers thrive in the country air.

Vegetables coexist in complete harmony with the flowers in the Camp garden. Tucked in among the rows is a house of sunflowers with a roof of morning glories which Edith Camp created as a playhouse for her grandchildren.

From the far end of the garden, the Camp's farm house, built in 1830, can be glimpsed through the trees.

One of the rooms in the Camp garden is shaped by beds of roses which flourish in this magical spot.

Located in the bluegrass horse country of Woodford County, Kentucky, the Labrot & Graham distillery (pages 92-93) was founded in 1812. Today it is the smallest distillery in the state, turning out limited batches of its Bourbon, Woodford Reserve. Great attention has been given to the landscaping of the grounds, as can be seen in the glorious daylilies lining the graceful curve of the drive.

Paths, Ponds, and Fountains

Down through the ages, from the very earliest gardens, the use of water as a decorative element has played a major role. Nothing is so soothing to the eye or ear as the sight of reflecting or playful water. To walk down a path and discover a peaceful pond or trickling fountain is one of life's unexpected pleasures.

The profusion of flowers bordering the garden path serves as a foil to the serenity and symmetry of the Perry pool.

(Above) The Ceci Perry garden in Lexington has a placid pool in the Palladian style. The precisely clipped hedge defines the pool's terrace and the weeping foliage behind is mirrored in the surface of the pool.

A stylized fish gently spouts an arc of water into the pool.

The aged brick path in the David Eager garden leads to the tool shed buttressed by clipped boxwoods.

Mrs. Henning Hilliard and her dog return from a morning's stroll in her garden to find a shady spot by the swimming pool.

The pool at Laura Lee Brown's Dogwood Hill is reached by a handsomely wide stairway. Lying well below the terrace, the pool cannot be seen from the house, a distinct advantage in winter when the cover is in place.

In the garden of Mrs. Robert McDowell Rodes in Lexington, this water nymph empties her urn into one of the garden's pools.

The swimming pool at Oxmoor is in a sheltered spot next to the house. The dark fringe-like foliage casts a cooling shadow on the water.

The dark finish of Helen Abell's pool makes it appear almost bottomless.

(Right) Located on the side terrace of the Abell house is a rectangular pool fed by three lion heads which peek out through the ivy.

(Left) Standing amid the roses, a little girl regards a small treasure in the Abell garden.

On a terrace in Jefferson County overlooking the Ohio River, a formal garden pool with its three fountains seems to float in a sea of green. The wrought iron railing, alive with vines and flowers, is a resting spot for birds and squirrels.

The curving upper terrace of this house on an Ohio River bluff provides an ideal area for entertaining.

The Stephen Clymer garden in Paducah, Kentucky, offers many enticing vantage points, including this inviting garden bench (right) overlooking a reflecting pond.

Mr. and Mrs. John Ross in Ashland have incorporated winding paths and lush ground cover to create an interesting flow through the garden.

Danville, Kentucky is the site of the garden of Mrs. Carlile Nichols. This ornate fountain and its trickling water are mesmerizing.

The waterfall gently running into the naturalized pond is a delightful area in Peggy Paxton's garden in Paducah.

Carp and koi enliven the Paxton's pond.

The Diane and Gary Klier garden in downtown Louisville uses the wall of the adjoining building as apart of the structure of the garden. Employing trellis fencing and a tall gate, the garden becomes a private sanctuary in the midst of a busy city. (Right) Raised stone edged beds and a curving path give the illusion of space and depth in the Klier garden.

Urban & Suburban Landscapes

The obstacles to be overcome by the urban gardener are great, but so, too, are the rewards. Challenged by lack of space, poor soil and acid rain, those who devote themselves to transforming brown fields into green ones are often the gardeners exhibiting the most creative designs and materials.

The Nichols garden in Danville has several paths leading out, giving the visitor a number of delightful choices.

(Left) The focus of Brenda Van Hoose's garden in Paris is on its small pond which is spanned by a delicate bridge.

The garden of Dawn Yates in Louisville presented a series of interesting problems. When Dawn purchased the property, nothing was growing there except two trees. A unique challenge was posed by a "heinous" concrete vault over fifteen feet tall which stores flood gates for the city. The flood wall runs the length of the yard. Meandering paths, vines, trees and mirrors intermittently placed along the wall create an almost tropical feeling.

(Left) This bust in the Yates garden seems to have become a part of this shady nook.

A sculptor, Yates finds inventive garden spaces to showcase both her own work and that of other artists.

Lounging in a rattan chair, Dawn steals a few moments to rest, surrounded by the glories of her city garden.

Lois Ann Polan is a garden designer in Lexington and what she has accomplished in her small, sloping backyard is testament to her extraordinary gift. The rear garden with its series of terraces is sculptural in approach. Water features and quiet resting spots offer islands of tranquility from the traffic beyond.

The view from Lois Ann's upstairs window encompasses the garden. She has suspended a pair of French doors and installed columns on the back of her neighbor's garage, adding depth and an odd touch of whimsy to her green and white garden. (Right) With more ideas than space, Lois Ann dug up her driveway and planted a rose garden bisected by a pea gravel path. Scattered among the pea gravel are clear glass beads called pilgrim glass. Each child who visits the garden is allowed to take one home.

The garden of Tom Schnapp and Billy Hertz is an extension of the Hertz Gallery in downtown Louisville. Sculptures large enough for a child to climb on, a bridge, a pond, and a circuitous path all contribute to a most unusual and welcome urban adventure.

A rust rooster tilts his head to crow, announcing a new day in the garden.

116

The water and the cooling trees seem almost forest-like, but one only has to glimpse the church steeple to be reminded that the Schnapp/Hertz garden is close to the city.

An aerial view of the Lauri and Howard Bledsoe garden in Old Louisville is but one of the ways to enjoy their well-executed plan. An oasis of trees and paths leading to inviting seats make it difficult to return to the world outside.

The Robert Webb garden in Paducah is home to this charming figure.

(Right) Old Louisville happily boasts a number of gardens in its midst. One of these is the garden of Irene Spicer. The lovely little pond and its trickling waterfall offer a spot in which to tarry for a few moments.

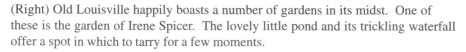

The Paul Grumley garden in Paducah has a distinctly classical feet with its immaculate brick walks, formal garden benches and stylish boxwood hedges. Though the city is close by, this garden could have been lifted out of England.

Jean and Sam Miller's garden is near one of Louisville's major thoroughfares, but once through the garden gate, the city is left far behind. This is the precious knot garden tucked beside the Miller's house.

The garden of Mrs. Robert McDowell Rodes in Lexington has been the recipient of several garden design awards.

The wrought iron gate in the Rodes garden opens into a petite ivy garden.

On the Rodes's patio, paving stones laid in concentric circles focus the visitor's attention on a column topped with trailing petunias.

Ellen Workman's garden in Hopkinsville, with its stone edge, curves gently toward a wooded area.

A well-placed bench assures a picturesque view of the alluring Workman garden.

Ellen Workman spends countless hours in her garden.

Narrow paths defined by beautifully tended boxwoods open on to expanses of grass bordered by flower beds created by Mary Jo Bowling at Twin Hollies.

A trellis in the Bowling garden provides an interesting backdrop for the roses.

(Left) The garden path at Twin Hollies Inn in Danville invites guests to linger along the stone path under the arbor shade trees.

The sundial in the Dr. and Mrs. John Lacy garden in Danville is the focal point for the beds of sun-loving flowers. The Carlile Nichols house overlooks the garden.

Mr. and Mrs. W. Pierce Paxton's garden in Paducah is engagingly terraced to draw the visitor down and around to view the garden and the glen beyond.

A rustic footbridge carries the eye across and through to the woods in the Paxton's garden.

Daylilies almost eclipse the sundial in the Paxton garden.

A window in Lucy Paxton's loghouse is framed by a lush window box.

A rabbit visits Ellen Workman's Hopkinsville garden.

Mr. and Mrs. Robert Garey's garden at the Fairway Inn in Paducah features a raised terrace which overlooks the golf course.

Ornamental wrought iron hangs against the trellis and is home to an array of potted plants.

This peaceful enclave graces the garden of Mr. and Mrs. Gene Katterjohn of Paducah.

Ken-Mill Place, the home of Mr. and Mrs. Paul Grumley, is a fine example of a boxwood knot garden.

A shady corner in the Ashland garden of Mr. and Mrs. John Ross shows the brilliant geraniums at their best.

The rest of the world is kept at bay in the walled garden of Mr. and Mrs. Cecil Fannin, Jr. in Ashland.

132

The Wallis House in Paris is the home of the Garden Club of Kentucky. Its garden features roses, daylilies and a lovely old arbor as well as one of the largest gingko trees in Kentucky.

Beth Garey lavishes special attention on her roses.

Grace Notes in the Garden

It is in the details of the garden where we discover the particular genius of each gardener. The choice of plant, flower or tree, the long-held preference for a certain tool, the placement of a statue, the siting of a pool or bench, all give the fortunate visitor a glimpse into the soul of these talented individuals.

Jane Welch in her caladium-covered straw hat spends a June morning working in her country garden.

The venerable arbor at Wallis House in Paris frames a pensive garden elf.

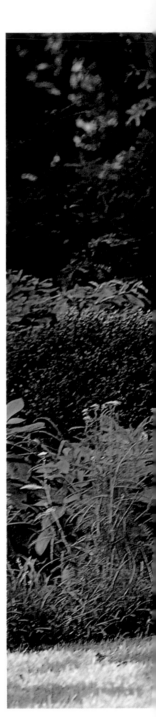

Watering cans are in constant use in the condominium garden of Mrs. Frederika Petter in Paducah.

Laura Lee Brown enjoys many hours in her garden tending myriads of details.

The demands of country gardening keep Lowrey Jackson of Boyle County on the move.

Vicki Prince ignores the heat and humidity of the Ohio Valley as she happily labors in her beautiful garden.

The garden of Mr. and Mrs. Ben Matthews in Shelby County is a study in perfection. Even Jean's workbench is worthy of a picture with its artfully arranged watering cans spouting Queen Anne's lace.

Cupid draws another arrow in the Matthews garden.

The acrobats in this eastern Jefferson County garden perform their aerial feats with the pool as their safety net.

A most unusual painted wrought gate opens onto the brick terrace of a Louisville home.

Cissy Nash is an indefatigable gardener whose artistic eye sees limitless possibilities. Her garden continues to expand each year and now includes an *orangerie*, rose garden, ornamental grass plantings, perennial gardens and a special section for her grandchildren. She says with a bemused expression, "It isn't really what we meant to do," but the effect is absolutely charming.

Each time Lilly, the Robert Nash's granddaughter, plays in the Longfield garden, she finds her likeness captured by Louisville sculptor Charlotte Price. The restaurant on Bardstown Road was named after her.

143

(Above) The pet cemetery at Oxmoor is the resting place for two centuries of the family's beloved horses and dogs.

The armillary in the Stephen Clymer's garden is a telling focal point in this very private garden.

Typical of Barbie Thomas's sense of humor is this decorative piece in her garden.

Casual in their arrangement but pure art in their very being are these hydrangeas in Lowrey Jackson's window.

Let us divide our labours, Thou where choice
Leads Thee, or where most needs, whether to wind
The Woodbine around This Arbor, or direct
The clasping ivy where it climb, while I
In yonder Spring of Roses intermixt
With Myrtle, find what to redress till noon...

John Milton,
Paradise Lost